GOTHIC BALLADS

IN DARKNESS THERE IS LIGHT

Sara Brunner

BookLeaf Publishing

India | USA | UK

Presentation by *BookLeaf Publishing*

Web: www.bookleafpub.com

E-mail: info@bookleafpub.com

ISBN: 9789358739176

First edition 2021

ACKNOWLEDGMENTS

I would like to say thank you to my nana. I truly appreciate you. Your support means so much to me. Thank you for giving me a life for all these years. I love you cookie.

I would like to say thank you to Anna. My dear, you mean the world to me. I wouldn't be writing or doing any of this without you. You are the best thing that has happened to me. I love you so much. I don't know where I would be without you. I truly appreciate you.

Thank you ink for supporting me and being my sister. I appreciate you for supporting me and my chocolate addiction.

And thank you to everyone on Instagram who has supported me and watched me grow. I appreciate all of you and hope to grow with all of you for many years to come.

DEDICATION

This book is dedicated to all those who are suffering silently in the night. Who feel they will never see the light again. Believe me when I say there is a way back, even when your rope feels like it is fraying. You are not alone. So hold on to that lifeline a little longer, you will find your beacon in the darkness. You are worth it, for no one can replace your soul. Someone is waiting for you and they will need you as much as you need them. It will get better, please do not give up. I hope these words can provide a sliver of illumination for you in the shadows as you begin your journey back to the living.

PREFACE

"In The Darkness I Know Myself"- Lithium by Evanescence

"Not All Who Wander Are Lost" – J.R.R Tolkien

I think I'm splitting once more

As the cracks in my foundation begin to shift

And my tears begin to pour

My mood changes so swift

Which version of myself am I now?

In the blink of an eye, I disappear

And my sanity takes a bow

Maybe this time it won't be so severe

Just close my eyes and breathe

Because I know my soul is still there underneath

I can't let the waves crash over me

Once more fighting back this maddening sea

Too sensitive I am

So I have such a hard time holding back that dam

Don't you see I am trying so desperately

And rationally, I know these feelings are only temporary

But to be in the eye of the storm

Drains every inch of me , makes me so worn

When you are at war with yourself

Then life's projectiles, you can't seem to propel

Slice into my brain, remove my past

For these memories weigh too heavily upon my soul

And I feel like I am walking on shards of glass

Losing myself in a world so cold

Falling to the demons of my past

Into my flesh, their claws have grabbed ahold

For in my mind, heaven and hell have clashed

And the prize, my heart to be sold

In front of me eyes all my sins have flashed

This Inferno, I have been bestowed

And in life, my existence has been recast

For my final show has just closed

Into my carotid artery, the blade has slashed

And this flow, can't be slowed

As the coroner has been dispatched

And into the oven, I have been enclosed

My walls may crack, and they may splinter

Call me evil, rip into my soul

But I won't be another causality in this winter

No, I won't disappear in your black hole

My humanity, that part of me, you killed her

And now this monster will rise

As the inferno takes over my eyes

My blood runs so cold

Now my new reality behold

As this hell starts to unfold

Down this surrealist nightmare we fall

As we hear the succubus's tempting call

Let the smoke turn your flesh into shadows

As your soul begins to become unknown

For you can't destroy what was already destroyed years ago

Don't you know insanity can't be controlled

As we continue our descent so far below

Welcome to my reality

As I continue to infect your bloodstream

Call out your god in blasphemy

For he can't save you now from my infectious disease

From this dream you can't awake, no you are not asleep

Nor is this fantasy

Forever caught between

Two worlds, for this is your fate

And now that hope you hold onto, it's too late

For all eternity you are trapped in this world I create

And to my creatures you'll be nothing but sheer bait

4.

I stand at this precipice of my life

Not knowing which direction to turn

I can't seem to take all this heartache, all this god damn strife

For the blood is always on my hands,

and into the fire I always seem to burn

This is my soul that is getting mutilated beyond repair

Yet the Gods don't seem to care

Let my tears flow, drain my fluids into the ground

Start to form my burial mound

Bury me while I'm still breathing

It's not like anyone will even hear my screaming

I'm been fading for so long, and now it's time to bid this dying body farewell

Don't you hear that melancholic death knell

Because in the end I don't know, if I was meant to be here

Just a random mistake, I fear

And to the suffering I give in

For I will let my descent begin

With open arms embrace the dark

As my body becomes the earth's sacrificial art

5.

It's ok not to be ok, to crack, crash and fall

To break into a million pieces

To not even be able to walk, only crawl

And no there isn't always a reason

Sometimes that darkness just takes over

Swallowing all that we are whole

As we slowly sink lower

Down that unending rabbit hole

Till all the light fades around us

And we feel like we are turning to dust

We are only human after all

And our hearts can stall

That dagger can cut into our veins, draining all our blood

And we can't seem to stop that flood

As we fall to our knees weeping

And into the floorboards that crimson keeps seeping

All the pictures in front of our eyes start to fade

And by the heavens we feel so betrayed

But we still can hold onto to that frayed rope

Because as long as we are breathing, we still have life

And even though we feel like our souls have broke

And all we can see is this venom tinged strife

There is still the scent of a new dawn in the air

Though we can't ever put back all the pieces, there is still enough to repair

From the suffering we can create a beautiful mosaic, that shines so bright

Under the rejuvenating moonlight

6.

Take a scalpel to my decaying brain

And please just slice away all the pain

I can't seem to win this internal war

I'm getting so tired paddling in this incessant ocean without
an oar

I'm losing myself once again in the fear

Taking control of my nervous system

As my insanity draws near

To all these shadows, I have become the victim

So scared I can't even breathe

For my hope, all I do is greive

Please someone grab onto me

I can't keep drowning forever in this sorrowful sea

With the bottom I will eventually collide

And that will be my slow demise

As the saline fluid fills my lungs

Into oblivion I fade from this life so young

But I'm not a ghost yet

So why do I keep having to pay all these debts

I never asked for any of this

And now it's my soul that is sinking into the abyss

Let my soul go up in this pyre

For the flames are only desire

Burn, witch, burn

For I'm going back from winch I

came

And I will never show any shame

I am not the one who sinned, so you can all be damned

Down my throat, your religion will no longer be crammed

The skies will weep for my death

As the smoke takes my last breath

But the ash and inferno will not stop me from being reborn

And your souls will not find salvation, you have been warned

For you are snuffing out a light

As pure as the newborn snow

And you will forever exist in a perpetual night

Well the torture you inflicted, will be your fate so far down below

So laugh and cheer at my demise

But out of the charred remains I will rise

Well you will be turned away at the gates

And every trace of your existence will be forever erased

And the deeds you committed, will become shunned

And no longer will humanity succumb

To fairy tales and fables that say who has sinned and who hasn't

Soon it will just be a part of history, a fragment

That we will no longer have an attachment

Do you know how fucking sick I am in, being locked up in this rusted cage

Binding me with your restraints

All I can seem to do that has any worth is bleed onto this page

I know you think that I can handle it all, but I'm not a goddamn saint

And I'm starting to lose control

In this dizzying whirlwind of hated

I think all the years have finally cracked me, took their toll

You don't like what I am becoming, well this is just the monster destiny created

Pushed to the brink for far too many years

With one foot always over the edge

Flooding the cavern below with all my smoldering tears

Not being able to find a way back from this jagged ledge

Cutting and tearing into my flesh, the damage has now become unrepairable

And I no longer hope for a miracle

For that is not my fate

The angels never came and now I fear it might be too late

I have no will left

For this existence took that, oh what a clever theft

Leave me barely breathing

Well the heavens among, on my prayers have been sleeping

And into the ether I will keep speeding

A cresudo of waves breaks against the shoreline

Dragging back everything it touches into the murky waters below

Only be laid to rest in life's saline brine

For mercy, did the universe forgo

It breathes life into us only to extinguish it again

Shatters us like a glass window pane

Slowly it extracts our hope, till our heart becomes slain

And into the watery depths of the cosmos we yearn to be

Bound by the harsh reality of everyday, we desperately try to flee

For the melancholic cries of the sirens sing out to our souls

And oh does that music sound so soothing, as all that you love erodes

Withers and slips through your now aged fingers

And every minuscule sound has now become a trigger

So let the cool water wash over our leathered skin

And fill our alveoli from within

As we lose conscious and our head begins to spin

And our journey into life everlasting begins

10.

Everytime I start to heal, I start to fall over that cliff again

No matter how hard I hold on, I begin to lose my grip

Oh god I'm plunging again, my hands are so bloody for my life being drained

Why did I have to fucking slip?

I tried very hard, can't you open your eyes and see

No this is not an optical illusion

Whatever the price for sanity I will pay thee

Because I'm dying in all this confusion

I can see my own demise, as I plumet in my final swan song

I know now this descent won't be long

Everything is whirling around my mind so fast

My whole life playing like a rebroadcast

All that I loved will be gone in a second

And to hell I will soon be at that desk, to check in

But don't cry for my deteriorating body

For even when I was alive, I was nothing but a mere zombie

So lay that pall over my coffin

And know that to a better life, over Styx's river, I will be crossing

The snows of uneasiness slowly fall around my dilapidated corpse

For my corporeal existence is no more

All that is left is a mere shadow bouncing off the decaying trees

As all that I once was is no more

Just a picture fading in people's fraying memories

Soon to even dissipate from the shores of time

Washed away like the melting snows of a new spring day

Just another long forgotten soul

Words that will smudge and disappear through the ages

On paper that will become so bitter and fragile

Cracking into a million pieces, only to become dust itself

Blowing away like smoke billowing from the fires of Tartarus

For nothing lasts forever and we all have an end date

So we try to go through this journey leaving as many marks as we can

But even those marks become illegible and weathered with the elements

Never knowing why or how we are actually here

Hoping that there is a reason to this madness

But truthfully we will never know

So everyday we wake up and hope that when we cross over all of this will make sense

But the irony is in order to know you have to die

So we live to die and die to live

Hoping the fabric of existence will be revealed before our opalescent eyes

Fear encompasses everything that I am, seeps into the very fabric of my being

Destroys the precious time I was given

For everyday I struggle to just walk through the mist of life

All I can hear seems to be these demons in my head

Ripping at me from within, try to crave their way out of my chest

Steal the still beating heart from out of my tired body

As my thoughts begin to race once more, pulling me under

Affliction is all I have ever known

For some of us are born into this world already scarred by the lives of our past

And into this reincarnation, meant to pay for those sins

From the nightmare of panic, we can not seem to wake

Living in a perpetual sea of adrenaline, that can not be quelled

So we drown again and again

Until we can no longer reach the shore once more

Sinking into the gloomy waters so far below

Until we become one with this disparaging sea

What do you fucking what from me?

The fates keep torturing my soul

Like I'm nothing but a rag doll to be tossed about

Keep ripping me apart, I'm sure I can take it

I have for so long anyway, it's not like a little more pain inflicted will do much damage

So push me to the brink

And then sit and watch me sink

Into this never ending pit of despair

Enjoy the show as I struggle to breathe, in this think arid air

Watch my limbs flail as I try to grab onto help

Laugh while the saline misery streams down my cheeks

A light of hope is all I seek

But into the eternal darkness my soul has been reserved

And I can never seem to find a way out

I am drowning in this dejected sea

While the universe plays chess with my destiny

But I never asked to be a part of this game

So my spirit from your grasp, please just release

And let me just fucking rest in piece

I sit here in pain again and wonder how much more can I bare

Before the fabric of my soul completely tears

How long can I live in this perpetual loop, before I become catatonic?

Because my conditions don't blow away like smoke, no they are forever chronic

Fuck it, they are damn demonic

I can't breathe in this storm, so cyclonic

Just the same revolving door, one after another

And all these voices, do smother

No I won't be fine, stop with your false pleasantries

Because what I have got, there are no earthly remedies

Complete insanity is my only plea

Because then from this purgatory I can flee

Living within the shadows of my past

And no matter how much I run, it is never enough

No, no matter how hard I try I am not that fast

And all the screaming, it just won't shut up

So my final descent has began

Into the Unknown I will wake up

And this can't be undone

So bid me farewell

As I give into this madness's spell

And my fleeting sanity I finally sell

Why do these words flow like a raging river, cut open my veins and watch the blood flow

As all that I lived through spills onto the paper beneath

Would my gift still exist without all my heartache

Without all the times I fell to the ground, that I broke

As my tears hit the floor like glass shattering into a million pieces

My breath being stolen by the demons that want to dance on my grave

As my world turns from dawn to a permanent dusk

And pieces of my soul float like dark clouds into space

Never to be seen again, vanishing into the nothingness of limbo

Would I feel this deep without experiencing the depths of hell

My childhood stolen and innocence lost

Leaving scars upon my heart and infecting my brain with this incessant voices of self hatred

Through you can't see these marks upon my flesh

They flood onto this canvas everytime the ink pours forth

16.

I'm not god and all this fucking pressure is starting to turn my soul so cold

My delicate heart that used to bleed is becoming stone

Hellfire is now flooding my eyes, as fury courses through my veins

I'm breaking these emotional chains

Soon I will become unrecognizable, as I shed this compassionate skin

And let out all that I held back so long from within

Oh my friend, don't you know everyone has the monsters in the dark, we are filled with sin

And now it's time for Beelzebub to win

You broke me, used me for the last time

Now let the apocalypse chime

Crimson oceans will spill

As I rip everything to shreds and go in for the final kill

For I am no longer human, don't you know you eviscerated that part of me so long ago

And now of this bloodlust I lost control

So I will sit back and watch the whole world burn

As back to the Dark Ages we return

And your bones will turn into ashes that I keep as a souvenir

in my precious collection of urns

Maybe I'm useless, worth nothing more than some words on this paper

As all that I felt and hoped for goes up on in some mist, mere water vapor

It's not like anyone saw me anyway

As I crumble to the ground once more like dried clay

Fading into dust, washing away with the putrid rain

All I ever did in this existence was cause irreparable pain

I swear I tried, to be a good person

But all I did was make every situation, worsen

For I felt too deep and the flood suffocated others souls

And onto my scarred heart, all this suffering took its toll

I don't even know if I'm whole

Shattering so many times there are not enough pieces to refill the mold

So for the final time I will fall down the rabbit hole

Disappear from this life

It's not like anyone will even notice I died

As my demons can no longer be denied

18.

Chaos comes in like a tornado sweeping you off your feet

You think you can outrun it, but hunny it will suck the life out of you

There is no escaping as the debris of your existence blows around your body

Grabbing out for the pieces but they swirl and break into nothing more than disintegrating memories

Just as fast as this maddening disaster comes, it goes

Leaving you broken and bloody sprawled on the ground

Calling out to the fleeting souls of your past

But even those reminiscent images won't last

Because we all end up alone, lost like celestial orbs floating around the infinity of the bleak universe

Desperately trying to cling onto the last bit of light

Before all our hopes gets extinguished like a fading flame in the night

For in the end we become nothing more than a name on a yellowing piece of paper

A brief encounter with the fates, just for a second in the grand scale of time

Before we disappear like grains of sand in the desert of annihilation

The darkness has become my friend to the point even the littlest light blinds

The ghouls slowly digging into my flesh, swallowing my slowly

But you can't see my plight, no this is an invisible fight

It's the monsters that crawl in my mind, and no it's not just in the dead of night

Every second I take a breath, it feels like I'm inhaling more of my inevitable death

Till I crawl even further into my rabbit hole, free falling till I can't even see the ground

For my fears are like a bottomless pit

And into my soul they are stitched in, into my heart knit

But these scars they leave no mark

And this ship I just want to disembark

Because it's the silence that kills me more

Living in the aftermath of my shattering,my own fucking gore

I know it's all in my head, I have heard this all before

But that doesn't make it go away, as my body once more hits
the floor

My eyes once more swelling and I'm not able to see though
the rivers flowing down my face

Please give me room, no hold me I can't take this blank space

Just make this pain go away, like this water drops on the
window pane, let it dissipate

Or at least from this nightmare let me finally awake

20.

I am losing who I am trying to become in this endless winter

My mind is beginning once more to crack and splitter

The white out of this Blizzard is obscuring my path

Mephistopheles is playing with my soul and I'm drowning in this colorless blood bath

Icicles of repentance are piercing into my delicate flesh

To this alabaster hell I have become enmeshed

An endless cycle of anguish, as my frozen blood no longer pours

For I have become this reality's whore

Why didn't I see the writing on the fractured wall?

Trying to fight Destiny was my ultimate downfall

I was meant to be a ghost, invisible to all of humanity

To forever live in my warped insanity

For everything I was and will be, always will be such a tragedy

I'm not meant to exist within normality

Now it is time for me to give into the the divine providence's brutality

And accept my bittersweet ivory fatality

Foresight is a razor wire curse, knowing only things the fates should

Feeling with such depth that every breath feels like your impending death

Maroon tears stream down your cheeks as your vision becomes so obscured

Your heart being crushed by the fears of the unknown

Because into your soul this murky "gift" has been sewn

And there is no escape, no matter how much you try to burn it out of your mind

Telling yourself over and over this can't be real, everything will be just fine

As the dreams intensify and the feelings become stronger

And you don't know exactly what is going to happen, but you know it can't be much longer

That impending doom is always attached to your back

Creeping up even in moments of calm, throwing you right back into that panic attack
Till your throat tightens and your are gasping for air

Because this uneasiness is too much to bare

Falling to your knees, pleading for the storm to not drag you away

But in this reality you don't know if you can really stay

The shadows are surrounding your shattered spirit as you lay in the fetal position, reaching out to the last bit of light in this demonic night

As you utter your last breath, you ask why did you have to give me the second sight?

All you hear as your candle gets blown out is because we thought you could handle that rite

The moonlight disperses as the blood flows down my chest

For I think my heart just broke for the last time and let go beneath my aching breast

My flesh is growing so snow white and I'm losing my sight

Oh god I can't even hear the sound of the birds anymore as I lose the glow of the fading light

To death I have just been betrothed

As my soul from my body begins to unrobe

All I can pray for is that there is something better on the other side

Because I can't take one more blow, I'm so sorry but I really tried

I don't think I was meant for this life
I've always been to sensitive

And every single word and action always plunged into me, being torn apart by fate's knife

But maybe that was my fault, my downfall for being so genuine

And now that silver cord has been severed
And to this earthen tomb I am no longer tethered
Upon my collapsing mind, there is no longer this pressure

And I hope that if I do find peace, I can float in that pool
forever

Swimming in that permanent Oasis, as I am no longer
wandering aimlessly through that extinct desert

Why does this soldering rain fall upon my deteriorating flesh?

I'm slowly burning alive and turning to ash

Pieces of my fallen existence are drifting away with the harsh winds of this suffocating inferno

I've been disposable all along, and now I'm fading into the terra forma

Just specks of dust that reflect for a mere second in the morning light

Only to dissipate as quick as they appeared

For I was never met to roam this realm, just another mistake that got forgotten about

A ghost floating around in an empty vessel

My soul was vanquished eons ago

And that heart that used to pump in my chest, withered into mere stone

Crumbling from an eternity of loneliness

For crimson rivers no longer pour through my veins

And those saline tears that used to stream down my sunken cheeks

Dried into a barren wasteland so long ago, even the memories have become lost in the static

And now I will become just another broken doll in the Devil's attic

As the last drop of color leaves my eyes and my endless suffering becomes so monochromatic

24.

I'm so worthless, I can't even defeat the voices in my head

Screaming out in the dark, crushing my will

No these phantoms are no longer my friends

And I can't control all the chaos will a little pill

The midst of despair shrouding my better judgement

And every bloody second feels redundant

Flashback after flashback, sinking into the tar pits of my
trauma

Until my heart pounds and this paranoia, I vomit

I can't seem to move forward, no matter how hard I try

I would give anything to know what it feels like to be normal,
any part of my soul the devil could buy

Because this is no life, this no longer is even survival

At death's gate in just awaiting my arrival

What is reality, what is truth anymore?
Do we really exist, because I have been here, lived all this
before

I know this door, seen this décor

Felt this fear in every pore

Are we doomed just to relive our past lives, repeat our
mistakes?

But this Existential dilemma I would like to forsake

Bow out into oblivion with no more retakes

25

As I sit here in my darkened room, lost in my failing thoughts

My demons come back to play with my nerves

Does anyone really listen, do you really read my words

In a world so cold, that can be sold and every soul bought

Am I just another fading voice lost in the void

Just to echo against the howling wind, only to disappear as fast as it came

After I bleed onto this tear stained paper, will the shadows really be destroyed

Or will I always live in this loop of never ending hopelessness, always the same

Does anyone really see the real me, all the scars that rest upon my heart

That I'm bleeding so profusely into my sorrow laden art

Or am I just another ghost evaporating into the background of a life so cruel

But existence is not rose colored
sunshine, it's so cruel

And we only live to be lost in the crowd

Till the day we are out six feet under the ground
Under the rain soaked clouds

Pouring down upon our burial mounds

For even our decaying bodies in the end get drowned

Because in the end, I don't think the heavens were ever really
around

26

No longer can I walk on this razor thin glass, without it cracking under my weary feet

The blood dripping onto the crystalline shards below

Slowly I'm being drained, don't you see that you're killing me, my heart is losing beats

And my aura is dissipating, losing its very essence, it's loving glow

Can't you see that I tried my best

Now all I long for is that eternal rest

I can only be beat down, torn apart so many times before the light goes out

As the citrine dawn becomes an obsolete perpetual dusk

But I did have some humanity once, I know that without a doubt

Along the way it must have faded and gingerly turned to dust

For now I've become nothing but this hollow shell

From being caged within this emotional cell

Are you not happy with what you see?

Don't you know that you made this ghost, you created this mourning, now with me you try to plea

There is no going back, I've killed all the empathy in my soul

And now you have to live with this monster that resides in what used to be my vessel

I've lost all my warmth, I hope you like to live in this frozen wasteland, where I have become so cold

Welcome to the Inferno, and we are in the last level

Forever freezing to death with the devil
Because in the end you destroyed what made me so unique, so special

What made me so sentimental, so very gentle

And now this endless torture is our shared fate, as your words shredded my heart and now our ending is so detrimental

What is wrong with me, can someone just flip the fucking switch on my brain

Because into this bitter winter's night, I am decaying under the harsh snow

I'm shattering like the ice, that is covering my soul

As the looming storms start to pick up around my freezing flesh

I'm going down in this white out

Pretty soon, I won't even be a memory, completely forgot about

The avalanche of memories burying what is left of me alive

And there is no way out, I'm losing oxygen, from this I can't survive

My breath is getting so shallow

My life is flashing before my eyes

But the constant fear I lived in made these visions so hollow

Because the demons would never die

And my life did just fly by, in the blink of my saline covered
eyes

I can the feel the life leave my bones

As I feel my heartbeat for the last time alone

Frozen forever in this place

With no way for my soul to find a way back to grace

28

Is this a gift or a curse, I can't tell what I am feeling

Is this just my anxiety or foresight?

And I'm drowning in these uncertainties

As the tears of the unknown wash over my soul

I can feel just enough to know something is wrong

But not enough to see the outcome

Clouded with the delusions of panic

And my heart is racing as my mind is going so manic

Losing sight of all that I'm trying so desperately to grab on too

I'm being dragged out once more into that rageful sea

As the tidal waves sweep me off my feet

The briny water choking my burning lungs

As my dread courses through my failing heart

The demons of my confusion ripping into my prefrontal cortex

My sanity sinking to the bottom of the ocean and being swept away by the tidal waves of trepidation

For this was never really a gift you see

And to the angels, I beg you to take this away, I plea

For I would rather live in utter oblivion

Then be tormented by always knowing that something lurks around that dark corner

For this has just been so insidious

And now I'm ready to just go, so I no longer have to live in this torture

29

My mistakes keep playing on repeat in this bed of nightmares from which I can't escape

For my poisoned roots have taken hold

Wrapping around my esophagus, and slowly burrowing into my throat

I never meant to be so toxic but my heart is decaying beneath this battered ribcage

Barely beating under this aching breast

My blood is turning so acidic, seering through my collapsing veins

Everyday losing more of who I was as my soul is chained to the memories of sorrow

Fading into the dusk as the light dims around my translucent face

No longer can I sustain life in this hollowed out place

I'm letting go, letting the roots take control
Slowly devour me whole

Sink into the thorns of despair

Asphyxiate on my last bit of stagnant air

For I'm beyond repair

And you really think the heavens will listen to my prayer

So let me sink into the decrepit earth

And begin my cosmic rebirth

30

I am Khaos, what I created can easily be destroyed

From life comes Death

We can all go back into the void

Snuff out our last breath

Go out like an asteroid

We came from dust

And if I must

This civilization I will readjust

Go up in flames, we will all combust

Ashes into the wind

Till the light becomes forever dimmed

For in the end we all sinned

And maybe it's time this earth gets skinned

Back to nothing but elements

For we were never that intelligent

Nor did we have that gentleness
It was all just negligent

And now it's time for our mass Exodus

* 9 7 8 9 3 5 8 7 3 9 1 7 6 *